BOYS VS. GIRLS: ARMAGEDDON

A one-act dramedy by
Adam J. Goldberg

www.youthplays.com
info@youthplays.com
424-703-5315

Boys vs. Girls: Armageddon © 2013 Adam J. Goldberg
All rights reserved. ISBN 978-1-62088-194-1.

Caution: This play is fully protected under the copyright laws of the United States of America, Canada, the British Commonwealth and all other countries of the copyright union and is subject to royalty for all performances including but not limited to professional, amateur, charity and classroom whether admission is charged or presented free of charge.

Reservation of Rights: This play is the property of the author and all rights for its use are strictly reserved and must be licensed by his representative, YouthPLAYS. This prohibition of unauthorized professional and amateur stage presentations extends also to motion pictures, recitation, lecturing, public reading, radio broadcasting, television, video and the rights of adaptation or translation into non-English languages.

Performance Licensing and Royalty Payments: Amateur and stock performance rights are administered exclusively by YouthPLAYS. No amateur, stock or educational theatre groups or individuals may perform this play without securing authorization and royalty arrangements in advance from YouthPLAYS. Required royalty fees for performing this play are available online at www.YouthPLAYS.com. Royalty fees are subject to change without notice. Required royalties must be paid each time this play is performed and may not be transferred to any other performance entity. All licensing requests and inquiries should be addressed to YouthPLAYS.

Author Credit: All groups or individuals receiving permission to produce this play must give the author(s) credit in any and all advertisements and publicity relating to the production of this play. The author's billing must appear directly below the title on a separate line with no other accompanying written matter. The name of the author(s) must be at least 50% as large as the title of the play. No person or entity may receive larger or more prominent credit than that which is given to the author(s) and the name of the author(s) may not be abbreviated or otherwise altered from the form in which it appears in this Play.

Publisher Attribution: All programs, advertisements, flyers or other printed material must include the following notice:
  Produced by special arrangement with YouthPLAYS (www.youthplays.com.)

Prohibition of Unauthorized Copying: Any unauthorized copying of this book or excerpts from this book, whether by photocopying, scanning, video recording or any other means, is strictly prohibited by law. This book may only be copied by licensed productions with the purchase of a photocopy license, or with explicit permission from YouthPLAYS.

Trade Marks, Public Figures & Musical Works: This play may contain references to brand names or public figures. All references are intended only as parody or other legal means of expression. This play may also contain suggestions for the performance of a musical work (either in part or in whole.) YouthPLAYS has not obtained performing rights of these works unless explicitly noted. The direction of such works is only a playwright's suggestion, and the play producer should obtain such permissions on their own. The website for the U.S. copyright office is *http://www.copyright.gov*.

COPYRIGHT RULES TO REMEMBER

1. To produce this play, you must receive prior written permission from YouthPLAYS and pay the required royalty.

2. You must pay a royalty each time the play is performed in the presence of audience members outside of the cast and crew. Royalties are due whether or not admission is charged, whether or not the play is presented for profit, for charity or for educational purposes, or whether or not anyone associated with the production is being paid.

3. No changes, including cuts or additions, are permitted to the script without written prior permission from YouthPLAYS.

4. Do not copy this book or any part of it without written permission from YouthPLAYS.

5. Credit to the author and YouthPLAYS is required on all programs and other promotional items associated with this play's performance.

When you pay royalties, you are recognizing the hard work that went into creating the play and making a statement that a play is something of value. We think this is important, and we hope that everyone will do the right thing, thus allowing playwrights to generate income and continue to create wonderful new works for the stage.

> Plays are owned by the playwrights who wrote them. Violating a playwright's copyright is a very serious matter and violates both United States and international copyright law. Infringement is punishable by actual damages and attorneys' fees, statutory damages of up to $150,000 per incident, and even possible criminal sanctions. **Infringement is theft. Don't do it.**

Have a question about copyright? Please contact us by email at info@youthplays.com or by phone at 424-703-5315. When in doubt, please ask.

CAST OF CHARACTERS

ABBY, she's a genius in France. (This play does not take place in France.)

BELLA, a ranking commander in the Girls' Liberation Army. Yes, her name is like Twilight, get over it.

DREW, a typographist and aide-de-camp to Guillermo.

GUILLERMO, General of Team Boys. A bad-boy who plays by his own rules, as opposed to the Geneva Convention.

HAT-TRICK, an enthusiastic soldier for the boys side. Best friends with Randy.

MARIE, a scientific genius for a fearful, superstitious world.

MCKENZIE, Princess General of the Girls' Liberation Army. But why does she do the things she does?

RANDY, a frustrated soldier for the boys' side. Why does no one take this seriously?

RETAINER #1, First retainer, best retainer. Female.

RETAINER #2, More like first retainer, worst retainer. Female.

SAMANTHA, a returning girl whose ambition and loyalty are constantly tested. Foe of McKenzie.

TERRY, a returning boy whose ambition and loyalty are constantly tested. Friend of Guillermo.

YVETTE, Abby's best friend. What she lacks in intelli-something, she makes up for in wanting it the most!

SCENE 1: THE BATTLEFIELD — BOYS' SIDE

(It's summer and it's war. Air raid SIRENS sound ahead of the curtain. At open, the stage is zig-zagged with jagged trenches. Various MIDDLE SCHOOL BOYS line this side: the girls must be off in the distance. The boys are in WWI regalia, heavy blue hats and blue trench coats. Every thing on the boy side of the war is blue, gray, or black. RANDY, shorter, leans against the barricade wall with his enthusiastic brother in arms, HAT-TRICK. The air raid siren fades.)

RANDY: It's always worse when the siren fades.

HAT-TRICK: Why, Randy?

RANDY: Because then you never know when it's going to go back on again. And it makes you realize you've gone deaf.

HAT-TRICK: What?

RANDY: And it makes you realize you've gone deaf!

HAT-TRICK: Didn't hear you. I was thinking about how loud the siren was. *(A beat.)* That's war, though.

RANDY: What is?

HAT-TRICK: This. With the trenches.

RANDY: I know that! War is all about trenches. With the trench coats and the trench foot and the trench...do you have a trench shovel?

HAT-TRICK: I don't, Randy.

RANDY: At least we can't dig any more trenches.

HAT-TRICK: That'd give us something to do. Before the next water balloon barrage.

RANDY: War is heck, Hat-Trick. War is heck.

(A pause.)

HAT-TRICK: It also never changes. I just want to make it home, so I can see your mother's face one more time.

RANDY: What?

HAT-TRICK: My mom! Ha ha, my mom's.

(SAMANTHA and TERRY enter, both around the same age. They're wearing typical kid's clothes; Terry in yellow with blue accents, Samantha in green with pink accents. They both have backpacks.)

TERRY: What's going on, Hat-Trick?

RANDY: *(Indicating Samantha:)* You can't be here!

HAT-TRICK: Things are goo— *(To Samantha:)* You can't be here.

SAMANTHA: Why not?

RANDY: Because she's the enemy?

TERRY: Sammy's the—   **HAT-TRICK:** Sammy's the—

HAT-TRICK: You go first.

TERRY: No, you, I insist.

HAT-TRICK: Why's Sammy the enemy, Rand?

RANDY: Well...she's a girl!

SAMANTHA: Thanks for noticing.

RANDY: And girls are the enemy!

TERRY: What?

SAMANTHA: Since when?

HAT-TRICK: *(Remembering:)* Oh yeah.

(Samantha and Terry look at him quizzically.)

There's kind of a war on. We have trenches.

SAMANTHA: And it's against the girls?

RANDY: They started it.

TERRY: Girls may be a tad...well, you know, girls, but I don't think they'd start a war.

SAMANTHA: Oh, like girls can't start a war if they want to?

RANDY: She's a saboteur. She's causing dissent already. Hat-Trick, show her a propaganda poster!

(Hat-Trick looks around and pulls out a poster. It's in the '40s Soviet style and reads: "Girls: Yuck.")

TERRY: Kind of a simplistic take on it.

SAMANTHA: Terry, this is idiotic. We are going to end this war thing, and—

RANDY: Oh, now you want to end this war? Just like a girl. Can't make up her mind.

SAMANTHA: Who asked you, Rand?

HAT-TRICK: She's right, Rand.

(Randy glares at Hat-Trick.)

For a girl, I mean.

(Samantha is about to speak up. Terry holds up a hand — "I got it.")

TERRY: *(Changing tack:)* So if there's a war, who's in charge of the boys? There is somebody, isn't there?

RANDY: Maybe.

TERRY: So there is.

RANDY: Maybe there isn't.

HAT-TRICK: Yeah, maybe the leader isn't. Whoops.

TERRY: Randy, who's the general?

RANDY: I can't tell you with an enemy spy present.

SAMANTHA: Randy D. Reynolds, if you want a clobbering—

TERRY: She'll do it, Rand.

RANDY: I won't crack under pressure.

(Samantha rolls up her sleeve.)

HAT-TRICK: She's rolling her sleeve up, Rand!

RANDY: It's Guillermo, okay? Guillermo.

TERRY: Guillermo Montego, or Guillermo Sawyer?

RANDY: I don't know, the one who always wears those jeans with the skulls on them.

SAMANTHA: Oh yeah, that's Guillermo Sawyer.

RANDY: If she ruins the war effort, it's on your hands, man!

HAT-TRICK: We won't be blamed for nothing!

(The SIREN goes back on; Randy and Hat-Trick stand ready. Terry and Samantha cross downstage, away from the trenches.)

TERRY: *(Louder:)* So, if he's the general of the boys' army—

SAMANTHA: Which I don't know why they need!—

TERRY: You're gonna need to, you know, look like a boy! So you can go undercover!

SAMANTHA: But I have—

TERRY: Let me look in my backpack!

(The siren cuts out.)

SAMANTHA: *(Too loud:)* That sounds!—that sounds...good.

TERRY: What?

(He takes out a boy disguise: a gray skater hoodie, a Sox cap, and a baggy pair of jeans.)

SAMANTHA: Those jeans are way too big. And they're stained.

TERRY: And?

SAMANTHA: Do you have a belt?

TERRY: Why would I bring a spare belt? I only need to use one at a time.

(He indicates his own belt. Samantha glares. Terry begins to search for something else; he finds a length of rope.)

TERRY: Happy birthday.

SAMANTHA: Glad you remembered.

(She puts on the ersatz belt and tries on the disguise. Everything droops, except the jeans, which are clinched tight.)

I look terrible.

TERRY: No, you look like you don't care. Which is good.

SAMANTHA: Do you know where Guillermo is gonna be?

TERRY: Not really.

SAMANTHA: And are you gonna ask for directions?

TERRY: Samantha. Can you at least *pretend* to be a guy?

(Beat. They trudge off. Blackout.)

SCENE 2: THE GENERAL'S TENT

(A small, crowded general's tent. There are more anti-girl propaganda posters: "Don't Think Pink," "Dragon > Princess," and "Smooched Lips Sink Ships." At a desk, tapping away at a typewriter, is the meek DREW. He takes dictation of GENERAL GUILLERMO, who's pacing.)

GUILLERMO: Dear Missus Hibbard. Read that back?

DREW: I want you to repeat everything I say. I want you to start another letter and write "Dear Missus Hibbard." Read that back.

GUILLERMO: I see you've done this gag before.

DREW: One of my favorites, general.

GUILLERMO: Alright. *(Returning to dictation:)* Blah blah blah, your son was horribly wedgied, the price of combat, "the ultimate evil of that accursed gender," then sign my name at the end. *(He pauses.)* And add some "Dulce et Decorum Est" to show I care.

DREW: You're an inspiration to us all.

(Terry enters. Samantha tries to follow, innocuously.)

GUILLERMO: Terry!

TERRY: Guillermo? Sup, man?

(They bro-hug and exchange an intricate fist-bump. It takes quite a while.)

Saw the tent from three blocks away. So what's all this war stuff?

GUILLERMO: Where you *been*? You missed the declaration and everything! The invasion of Chester Drive!

TERRY: I just got back from a theme park, man!

(Drew looks up at Samantha, who just waves politely.)

GUILLERMO: Twisted Terrace?

TERRY: Even better. Arroyo Hills.

GUILLERMO: That is sick. Did you go on the Twistawhirl?

TERRY: Only six times!

SAMANTHA: Only twice, more like.

(Terry throws her a sour look.)

GUILLERMO: Who's that?

TERRY: Oh, that's my friend Sam. He's *really shy*, so don't worry about him.

SAMANTHA: Yeah? *(A beat.)* I'm wicked shy.

GUILLERMO: Oh. Well, alright.

SAMANTHA: So why'd the war start?

GUILLERMO: The girls engaged in biological warfare.

TERRY: Whooping cough? Measles? Le Grippe?

DREW: Cooties.

TERRY: Wow. They *weaponized* it?

GUILLERMO: *(Pronouncing "Marie" as in "Curie":)* Absolutely, maggot. That Marie Eggmond girl was working on something, and everyone started getting sick. But only boys.

SAMANTHA: Marie would never —

TERRY: I am NOT a maggot.

GUILLERMO: It's just a saying, grunt. No big.

TERRY: Anyway, I thought cooties was just a myth! Like if you don't find anyone to take to prom, you hafta take your sister.

SAMANTHA: I've never heard that before.

DREW: Wait, what if you don't have a sister?

GUILLERMO: Wait, what if you're a girl?

DREW: What if you want to take your sister, but then you *would* have someone to take, so you couldn't, but—

> *(Everyone stares at Drew after this one. A beat. He smacks his typewriter back into position with a loud DING.)*

SAMANTHA: So we're just at war with the girls now? Forever?

GUILLERMO: I don't know how long this war will take. But it's only war that brings peace.

SAMANTHA: Umm, only peace can bring peace.

GUILLERMO: I don't know if I like your new friend, Terry. He's not very good at being shy.

TERRY: Sam has a point, though. What if we...what if we found Marie, and had her engineer a cure?

SAMANTHA: Or got the girls to have a peace talk?

GUILLERMO: Peace talks would be excellent. While we had them, I could flank their entire army.

TERRY: So we could—

GUILLERMO: But do *not* tell them I'm surrendering. You have to get *them* to the table first.

TERRY: Ah, man.

GUILLERMO: Hey, if you don't like it, we could always use more cavalry.

SAMANTHA: Calvary?

GUILLERMO: All you need is a shopping cart, we provide the broom. Just make sure it's not one with the wheels that lock when they leave the parking lot.

(No response from Terry.)

We learned that the hard way. Open offer, maggots.

(Drew's typewriter DINGS. Blackout.)

SCENE 3: THE GIRLS' CAMP

(The scene starts a bit downstage, with upstage in darkness. All that's around is a convenient shrub. Samantha has returned to her more feminine green and pink ensemble.)

SAMANTHA: So we've got to talk to the girls. *(A beat.)* Do you have a clue where they're located?

TERRY: No. Why don't you ask a girl?

SAMANTHA: *(Sarcastic:)* Because they're just *marching* around —

BELLA: *(Off:)* Samantha Shockley!

(Terry hides behind the shrub. Samantha whirls around. BELLA enters. She's flanked by two girl guards, ABBY and YVETTE. All three of their outfits are pink and green camo with floral patterns, with a 1970s jungle-warfare theme.)

Samantha, this doesn't look good for you.

ABBY: Not at all.

YVETTE: Oh no.

BELLA: You're in for it.

SAMANTHA: In for what? —

BELLA: Caught in the DMZ.

SAMANTHA: What's that?

ABBY: De "militarized zone."

BELLA: Not in uniform.

YVETTE: Not even a *little* bit in uniform. Like, a hat.

ABBY: Or camo eyeliner.

SAMANTHA: I was...I just got here. I didn't know there was a war.

BELLA: Ignorance is no excuse!

YVETTE: If everyone knew why they were fighting, do you think we'd even *have* wars?

SAMANTHA: So where can I get an outfit?

BELLA: It's too late for that, whelp.

YVETTE: Yeah.

ABBY: Whelp!

YVETTE: Whelp!

BELLA: You're coming with us.

SAMANTHA: *(Feeding info to Terry:)* To meet your leader?

BELLA: Absolutely. *(Trying the phrase on for size:)* Wuh-help. Whelp. Now it just sounds weird.

SAMANTHA: If that's what you think is best.

BELLA: Then come with me. *(Confidentially, girl-to-girl:)* I've been patrolling in these boots for half an hour and they're completely grody. And there are *boys* around here.

ABBY: You should've seen what they did to Chester Drive.

YVETTE: It looks like Buzz Lightyear had a monster truck show.

(They march Samantha upstage. She drops her backpack. Terry looks at it. Crossfade to upstage.)

(The Girls' Headquarters is almost regal, clearly based on a medieval war room. On a throne is princess MACKENZIE KING. She wears a tiara and a regal dress; the only nod to her military nature is camo eyeliner. She's admiring herself in a mirror, knitting her own heraldry. A pair of RETAINERS go

over a map, moving military figurines over a battlefield.)

RETAINER #1: If we lose the Snack-Mart, our entire eastern front will collapse.

RETAINER #2: There are other ways to get sugar, Lucy. You're blinded by your love of ring-pops.

RETAINER #1: Sorry, little miss "tactical retreat." If it were up to you, we'd win the war by surrendering! Boys are aggressive and lousy and your tactic is to run away!

RETAINER #2: We've lost a lot of good girls there, OK?

(She looks far off into the distance.)

How do you ask someone to be the last girl waterballooned for a mistake?

(Retainer #2 storms off.)

RETAINER #1: Kelly, I didn't—

(Retainer #1 follows her. Bella, Abby and Yvette enter after, escorting Samantha.)

BELLA: Good news, princess-general!

MCKENZIE: Princess McKenzie is fine. Or Princess King.

ABBY: Yes Princess King.

SAMANTHA: *(To herself:)* McKenzie...

MCKENZIE: Who did you bring in? A new recruit?

BELLA: Worse, my liege. A...a deserter.

SAMANTHA: No I'm not.

MCKENZIE: Oh my god.

SAMANTHA: It's...

MCKENZIE: You?

SAMANTHA: You're the head of the girls?

MCKENZIE: The Princess Executor of The Girls' Liberation Army, yes.

YVETTE: You tell her, Queen Execut...Queen Exec...

ABBY: Head executive of the Princess Libertarians.

YVETTE: Thank you, Abby.

ABBY: Thank *you*, Yvette.

> *(They giggle. Bella and McKenzie both silence them with tandem withering looks.)*

BELLA: I assume you know the captive?

> *(McKenzie stands up, starts pacing around Samantha, sizing her up. After a moment of this, Samantha begins counter-circling McKenzie. The dialogue continues as they go around in circles.)*

MCKENZIE: So.

SAMANTHA: Yep.

MCKENZIE: Thought you'd show your face around here, *boy liker*.

SAMANTHA: Your goons dragged me here, "princess." I don't think war is the answer.

MCKENZIE: They started it! They're the ones—can we stop for a second? I'm dizzy.

SAMANTHA: *(Calculating:)* Sure.

> *(They both stop pacing.)*

MCKENZIE: Where was I?

BELLA: "They started it."

MCKENZIE: They did start it! The boys. They're —

SAMANTHA: How? They say Marie Eggmond weaponized cooties.

(Yvette and Abby gasp. Terry, dressed comically as a girl, takes this moment to walk in. He observes the silence for a second.)

TERRY: *(Sotto:)* Whoops. I was just...forget it.

(He leaves.)

BELLA: *That* is what we're fighting for.

MCKENZIE: *(To Samantha:)* "They" say? Who's they?

SAMANTHA: Boys.

MCKENZIE: So you talked to boys?

SAMANTHA: I have my...sources.

YVETTE: You *are* a boy liker.

ABBY: Boy liker! Boy liker!

YVETTE AND ABBY: Ewwww.

(They giggle.)

SAMANTHA: General Guillermo says that he's willing to make peace, if you hand over the scientist and admit wrongdoing.

MCKENZIE: Gu...Guillermo said that?

(She pauses a second.)

I don't care what he says anymore. He had his chance to do me right, and he —

SAMANTHA: "Do you right"?

MCKENZIE: Silence! Let me think.

(She begins pacing, laterally now. She turns to Bella, Yvette and Abby.)

You can leave any time.

BELLA: Yes commander!

(She salutes and marches offstage.)

YVETTE: Yes commander princess!

(She salutes and marches off stage.)

ABBY: You've got it... *(Abby searches for the phrase:)* Sir!

(She marches off.)

MCKENZIE: Heavy is the head that wears the tiara.

(She returns to her throne.)

Surrender is out of the question. If you want to investigate the good doctor, you can find her in her lab.

SAMANTHA: And where's that?

MCKENZIE: Deep in boys' territory. Under the Rebaron's doghouse.

SAMANTHA: Red barons?

MCKENZIE: Rebaron. Scotty?

SAMANTHA: Oh, sure. See you later?

MCKENZIE: As if.

(McKenzie laughs. Samantha stares, not very clear about the answer.)

You reverse engineer that formula, and we'll talk.

(She goes back to her heraldry. Samantha leaves. As she does, the light comes back on to Terry, still changing.)

SAMANTHA: Fat lot of help you were.

TERRY: So what'd you learn?

SAMANTHA: Just follow me, Tootsie. *(Mumbling:)* See if I ever get captured again—

TERRY: You're just jealous, cuz you *know* I look good.

   (Blackout.)

SCENE 4: BACKYARD/MARIE'S LAB

(Terry and Samantha check the coast. It's clear. The yard itself is fairly limited; the only major set piece is a red doghouse on the stage bonnet, and a few scattered chew toys. The Doghouse is cut out in back, and opens into offstage, allowing actors to re-enter into the upstage lab.)

TERRY: Ladies first.

SAMANTHA: Thank you. *(She pauses.)* You know the phrase "someone's in the doghouse"?

TERRY: No. Not really.

SAMANTHA: It means they're in trouble.

TERRY: Ah.

SAMANTHA: But what if you're a dog? It'd be good to be in the doghouse.

TERRY: Well wouldn't it be better to be in the people house?

(A beat.)

SAMANTHA: I guess you're right.

TERRY: Try not to crawl on the chew toys.

(Samantha and Terry crawl into the doghouse, emerging in Marie's lab.)

(Marie's lab is a junkyard carnival. Everything is repurposed, burbling and/or buzzing. A messy cot is in the corner. Food is scattered about. MARIE is working at a bench, mixing reagents. She doesn't notice Samantha and Terry.)

MARIE: Too much sodium, and it won't explodium. *(She thinks for a moment:)* Is it, not enough sodium, boils your throatium? I hate chemistry.

SAMANTHA: Hi, we're...

(Marie whirls on the pair, wielding an Erlenmeyer flask like a club.)

MARIE: Intruders! Well, I'll have you know, I'll never work for you. And my research plans cannot be decoded by your inferior ape brains.

TERRY: *(Peering at a diagram:)* Clearly. Is this upside down?

MARIE: Don't touch that! Get your paws off it!

TERRY: Wow.

(He gives a "What is wrong with her?" look to Samantha, who laughs.)

MARIE: Stop exchanging data facially!

SAMANTHA: What? You are Marie Curious, right?

MARIE: No. I am D'Marie Eggmond.

TERRY: "D"? What's "D"?

MARIE: It is very short for doctor. I am a post pre-pre-pre-Doctor of Physical Anthropology.

TERRY: Sorry, D'Eggmond.

MARIE: Apology accepted. You surely didn't know any better.

(Terry takes a deep breath, trying not to say something he would regret. This takes considerable effort.)

SAMANTHA: Me and my friend Terry—

(Terry gives a terse wave.)

—just want to find out why you weaponized cooties.

MARIE: What?

SAMANTHA: We want to find out—

MARIE: I heard that part! No, I would never do something like *that*. Where would I even get a sample of cooties?

SAMANTHA: From a boy?

MARIE: Oh! No, of course. I have a boyfriend up in Canada actually.

SAMANTHA: *(Yeah, right:)* What's his name?

MARIE: B...Bustin...Bustin Jieber.

(Terry cracks up laughing at this. Samantha smiles but keeps composed.)

Stop laughing at me, you, you simian! You...

(Marie returns to her experiments. She turns over her shoulder:)

Is that why you tracked me down? Because you think I'm a weirdo scientist?

TERRY: You live under a doghouse.

MARIE: I...

(She shuts down completely, refusing to even look at the pair.)

It was *definitely* "too much" sodium.

(She begins pouring from another beaker.)

SAMANTHA: Marie, wait. Terry didn't mean to imply that you were a crazy psycho.

MARIE: Hmm?

SAMANTHA: We totally don't think that.

TERRY: That's only like five percent of it.

(Samantha elbows Terry.)

SAMANTHA: We just want to know...if you didn't do it, what started the war?

MARIE: War is a negative urge, created by boy and girlkind's need to assert themselves.

TERRY: Here we go.

MARIE: War is the unbridled hubris of an entire species, and it manifests not as a matter of politics, but as a matter of...of...of simple existence!

SAMANTHA: I am 100 percent, completely...not following you.

MARIE: War created itself!

SAMANTHA: Then why hasn't it happened to kids before? Why doesn't it happen all across the country?

MARIE: Well...follow me to the sketch board.

(Marie motions over to a giant doodling pad. She draws as she talks.)

Now, consider powerful actors. Politicians. Well-liked people. Give me an example.

SAMANTHA: Like the school board president?

MARIE: Smaller.

TERRY: A toy model of the school board president?

MARIE: You mock me with your insolence! No, someone at our level.

SAMANTHA: McKenzie King.

MARIE: Ah, yes. She...

(She begins to draw a giant circle, labeled with a crown.)

Would attract a crowd of underlings. This is called the cult of personality. Powerful leaders draw people to them, including tacticians, bodyguards, and... *(Under her breath:)* Scientists.

Boys vs. Girls: Armageddon

TERRY: What was that last one—?

MARIE: The compounds were unstable and besides I would not do it! Cooties can not be weaponized!

(She begins scribbling all over her diagram.)

It is spread in a one to one ratio! She was foolish to have even asked!

SAMANTHA: So McKenzie asked?

MARIE: Non. I will say nothing else on the subject.

SAMANTHA: Come on.

MARIE: No way. I may be smart, but I'm not stupid.

(She pauses, then cleans up the doodle pad.)

Now, consider a male figure. One whose power is equal to hers. Someone with magnetism. A real dreamboat.

TERRY: Guillermo.

MARIE: It could be anyone! But yes. Now, imagine they coalesce, and break up, perhaps very publicly, perhaps outside the Hoopty Burger on Chester Drive...

SAMANTHA: Everyone would choose a side.

MARIE: Hypothetically!

TERRY: All the boys picked Guillermo, 'cuz he's awesome, and all the girls were stuck with McKenzie.

MARIE: Even a dullard like Goodall could've predicted that. Too many chimps in the kitchen.

TERRY: So all this was...was about a lover's spat?

MARIE: It is never that simplistic! But yes, entirely.

SAMANTHA: So we could end the war by getting them

together?

MARIE: That is *très* impossible. If I know McKenzie, she'll never leave her tent.

(A beat.)

SAMANTHA: Unless...unless it were for a treaty.

TERRY: Samantha, you're brilliant.

MARIE: No, *I'm* brilliant!

(She indicates a BUZZING machine.)

I bet you can't even tell what this does! Well, I *built* it!

TERRY: What's it do?

MARIE: Well, it beeps when it buzzes. And it lights up when it beeps.

(On cue, the machine BEEPS, BUZZES, and lights up.)

Good—it works.

SAMANTHA: Marie, what if I told you I had an idea for a sociological experiment?

MARIE: I'd listen to you.

SAMANTHA: What if...

(Samantha scribbles it down. Marie grins.)

MARIE: I'll head right on over. Just make sure that they arrive.

SAMANTHA: I will.

(Samantha extends her hand for a high five. Marie throws out the symbol for scissors.)

MARIE: Scissors. I win.

(Samantha sighs.)

TERRY: Your beeper stopped buzzing.

MARIE: Then you should go. Now.

(Marie rushes to fix her machine. Terry and Samantha rush to escape. Blackout.)

SCENE 5: ROMANTIC PORCHLIGHT

(It's evening now. The sun dawdles in the sky. Guillermo, Terry and Drew sit on one side of a picnic table. The table has a white tablecloth and a candle in the center. Across from them sit McKenzie, Bella, and Samantha. Abby, Yvette guard the perimeter from one side. Randy and Hat-Trick guard the other. Bella tries to intimidate Drew, who sizes her up quizzically. The game of this scene is trying to corral an awkward, awkward postbreakup chat into a peace treaty. It's the most personal problem that concerns the broadest possible consequences, but at the same time, extremely human.)

TERRY: Thank you both for coming. It takes a big...person...to come to the table in honesty.

(The next lines are high-stakes small talk.)

GUILLERMO: Uh-huh.

McKENZIE: Yup.

GUILLERMO: Yeah.

MCKENZIE: Uh-huh.

(They both pause.)

GUILLERMO: Yup.   **MCKENZIE:** Yup.

(The male and female underlings strive for decorum.)

BELLA: We refuse to surrender.

SAMANTHA: It's not a surrend—

DREW: We do too.

MCKENZIE: How are you doing, Guillermo? How's your pet frog?

GUILLERMO: Good as always. You're looking great, *bella*.

BELLA: Me?

    (Nope, not her; the Italian word. Bella face-faults.)

MCKENZIE: Thank you.

GUILLERMO: I thought you didn't like Mudsy.

MCKENZIE: *(Breezily:)* I don't.

GUILLERMO: Oh.

    (Samantha and Terry look at each other. Marie, dressed as a waiter, enters upstage, carrying a picnic basket. She lays it on the table.)

MARIE: Bon appétit.

    (She exits.)

BELLA: *(Automatically:)* It's poisoned.

TERRY: It's not poisoned. *(To Samantha:)* Is it poisoned?

SAMANTHA: It's not poisoned. It's hot dog.

DREW: *(Grammar snob:)* They're hot dogs. And they're poisoned.

SAMANTHA: OK, I don't know where everyone gets off thinking they're poisoned, but if you want to eat one, I'll eat one. Because they aren't.

DREW: Fine by me.

    (They both take a hot dog out. Cautiously, they both fake a bite.)

Mmm.

SAMANTHA: That's good!

MCKENZIE: *(To Guillermo:)* You made *me* hot dogs, remember?

GUILLERMO: On the grill, yes. Avocado, ketchup, mustard, toasted bun.

MCKENZIE: I had three.

GUILLERMO: You had four, but who's counting?

(They both laugh in a lovebirdy way. Everyone else sighs a breath of relief. Samantha tries to offer a packet of forms to Drew.)

SAMANTHA: You'll see the terms are quite reasonable.

DREW: Maybe.

(They try to ignore Guillermo and McKenzie, who've started feeding each other potato chips. McKenzie dips one in coleslaw.)

TERRY: *(Re: the contracts:)* They're certainly neutral.

BELLA: Do I get a copy?

GUILLERMO: Oh, pooky.

(Terry gives Bella a copy.)

MCKENZIE: Oh, Gilly.

BELLA: Odd that you had two.

TERRY: You gotta complain about everything, huh?

BELLA: Maybe I do.

SAMANTHA: He was just saying.

BELLA: Alright, OK. *(Defensive-aggressive:)* Maybe I don't.

DREW: General, if you could just sign here...

(He passes the document and a pen over to Guillermo, who scrawls absentmindedly.)

BELLA: Everything seems alright, McKenzie, if you'll just...

(McKenzie signs off as well.)

GUILLERMO: You're the darling of my eye. My morning laugh.

MCKENZIE: You're the parapet of my castle.

GUILLERMO: Oh, you're still doing the princess thing? For real?

MCKENZIE: What do you mean, for real?

GUILLERMO: Well, for one, you're a princess and you hate my frog!

MCKENZIE: I kissed you before, and *you're* a frog!

SAMANTHA: Well that's plenty, we ought to be going...

GUILLERMO: What do you mean, I'm a frog? You're as spoiled as vintage milk!

MCKENZIE: Oh yeah?

GUILLERMO: Yeah, times a million!

MCKENZIE: I'm done with you!

GUILLERMO: Drew, tell her I'm done with her.

DREW: General McKenzie, he's done with you.

MCKENZIE: Oh, he can't say it himself?

(Guillermo grabs his copy of the treaty, ripping it in half. McKenzie rips up hers. They and their entourages leave, leaving Terry and Samantha alone at the table. Marie comes back with a second picnic basket.)

MARIE: Ah. I predicted this.

TERRY: No you didn't!

MARIE: I only have three cupcakes.

(Terry checks the picnic basket. He frowns and takes them out;

three cupcakes.)

SAMANTHA: We can try again. There's got to be a —

BELLA: *(Off:)* We've been flanked!

GUILLERMO: *(Off:)* Ever hear of a contingency plan? To arms!

(The SOUNDS OF BATTLE erupt.)

MARIE: *This* is the price of leaving one's lab. No good science goes unpunished.

TERRY: Samantha, what do we do? We can't just try again. There's...maybe Marie was right.

MARIE: Of course I was! *(A beat.)* About what?

TERRY: War being inevitable. If popular people want it to happen, it's going to.

SAMANTHA: But the reasons are so petty. It's over...it's over a frog! Not even over the frog itself, but how McKenzie feels about it!

(Terry absorbs this, saying nothing. Marie simply motions for Terry to continue. She eats a cupcake through the following argument.)

TERRY: It's never about the reasons. It's...people are eager to fight. That's what they get every day — action figures and video games and the news...

SAMANTHA: You aren't *blaming* those things?

TERRY: But what about what they create? Exposure! Programming! All that junk! We're in a war culture.

SAMANTHA: People can be better than their culture.

TERRY: Since when?

SAMANTHA: Since art! Since music! Since the invention of frosting on cupcakes!

(Marie, thinking she's implicated, stops chewing.)

TERRY: So we can —

SAMANTHA: Since *amusement parks*! There's nothing violent about going in a loop on a steel track. There's nothing violent about a Ferris wheel or a water slide or a ring toss —

TERRY: Or a shooting gallery?

(Samantha pauses, reflects. Another pause.)

SAMANTHA: So do you surrender to it? Do you think of people as better than they could be? Terry, do you honestly believe in peace?

TERRY: What's the point if I'm the only one who does?

(Pause. Samantha holds his hand.)

Or if it's just me and you.

SAMANTHA: I don't want to be on opposite sides because of something stupid.

TERRY: But why do people fight?

SAMANTHA: Because they can?

(This sparks something in Terry. He kisses Samantha on the cheek, and leaves without a word. Samantha doesn't speak. Marie puts a hand on her shoulder.)

MARIE: Cupcake?

SAMANTHA: He's...he's right, though. I think. Sure.

(They munch on cupcakes for a second, lost in thought.)

What happens with no leaders?

MARIE: You cannot be suggesting—

SAMANTHA: What would happen?

MARIE: Well, speaking *purely hypothetically*—

SAMANTHA: Just tell me.

(Marie pauses, flabbergasted.)

MARIE: Chaos. Destruction. Cats dressed up as dogs.

SAMANTHA: So what's the solution? You're smart, tell me.

MARIE: A new leader could potentially—

SAMANTHA: Fill the void.

MARIE: Stop interrupting me?

(Samantha shrugs "sorry.")

Of course, there are potential consequences.

SAMANTHA: Always are. For doing what's right, I mean.

(Marie snickers at the word "right.")

Oh?

MARIE: Nothing. I'm going to ground. What if McKenzie didn't believe the waiter disguise?

SAMANTHA: McKenzie won't be a problem much longer.

MARIE: You're...

(Marie smiles, getting it. Then frowns.)

SAMANTHA: It's not *about* want-to. It's about have-to. One day, this war's gonna end.

MARIE: Better girls than you have said that.

SAMANTHA: Not loud enough.

(Samantha exits, determined. Blackout.)

SCENE 6: THE GIRLS' CAMP

(McKenzie is on the throne, teary eyed. The Retainers are back, pointedly not speaking to each other, moving miniature armies around on their maps. One moves a division; the other moves it back. Glares. Samantha enters. McKenzie blows her nose with a honk.)

SAMANTHA: Are you announcing me?

MCKENZIE: I...

(She blubbers.)

SAMANTHA: Oh, girl up.

MCKENZIE: What do you, *(Sniff.)* want?

SAMANTHA: Victory. How could those boys do this to you?

MCKENZIE: Could...to me?

(Samantha waves for the Retainers' attentions. They look over. She points toward the left. They exit left.)

SAMANTHA: Guillermo thought up that whole peace treaty thing to trick you.

MCKENZIE: No he didn't. He was...he was...he had good intentions. He's a good person.

SAMANTHA: Do you believe that?

MCKENZIE: I don't know what I believe.

SAMANTHA: Believe in me.

(She pats McKenzie on the back.)

You can't believe in boys. Or even men. They get what they want and they walk right out on you. You loved him, and he whined about some frog. What you need is a battle plan.

MCKENZIE: A... *(McKenzie thinks for a moment. She appears* *swayed, then:)* It... *(The great dam of McKenzie breaks:)* Lana Buchannon had been teasing me, for weeks. And this was just after I had moved to a new school. She tormented me, the worst kinds of names—the names you don't repeat, trashing my locker on a daily basis, and...I told Guillermo Sawyer. Who sat next to me in math. And he says not to even worry about it, and how tears—how tears messed up my gorgeous face!—how he wouldn't even...just not to worry about it.

SAMANTHA: Lana was expelled for pulling the fire alarm three days in a row. —You didn't.

MCKENZIE: *(Through her tears:)* It was beautiful! That he would—

SAMANTHA: She had to *move*.

MCKENZIE: How am I supposed to go to war? With someone who would do that for me?

SAMANTHA: You don't go to war. You win.

(Samantha moves over to the maps, still processing the Lana story.)

MCKENZIE: It would make us equal. He stands up for me when I need him, and I...and I forgive him. I forgive him everything. That's love, isn't it? When you shut up and let the other person win.

(The words hang.)

SAMANTHA: Can you even hear yourself?

MCKENZIE: Of course I can hear myself. I can hear my heart beating in my ears and it's like my name carved into an oak tree.

SAMANTHA: And the frog? Is the frog in the oak tree?

MCKENZIE: You don't get it! You just don't...

SAMANTHA: We take back Chester Drive.

MCKENZIE: We what?

SAMANTHA: We marshal every girl in town and we take back the block. The Hoopty Burger, the gas station, the playground with the big ditch and the one slow swing set—

MCKENZIE: *(With low cunning:)* How do you know it so well?

SAMANTHA: I just do. I keep up to date on—

MCKENZIE: You wouldn't know about the swing set, unless you lived there for a while.

SAMANTHA: I want to save our gender, and you—

MCKENZIE: This is about you! This is about you taking an entire war...taking everyone!—and getting what you need out of it. Just to get your house de-occupied of boys.

SAMANTHA: *(Half threat:)* And what if that's true? Are you gonna send Bella after me? You were about to surrender, what if I tell her that?

MCKENZIE: I...

SAMANTHA: So we'll do it?

MCKENZIE: I don't even know if it's right anymore.

SAMANTHA: It's war. No one does. And that's really not the point.

> *(McKenzie isn't convinced. We see a change in Samantha; whether she's buying into what she's saying or not is now extremely hard to tell.)*

Think of every girl you know. Think about what it'd be like if the girl they respected, the one they all chose in the breakup, was to roll over and let a boy win. That's what you'd be asking them to do with *peace*.

MCKENZIE: So it's...

SAMANTHA: War, McKenzie. Ultimate, complete, total war. On the street where it all began. And yes, maybe I live there. But that just means I know what it takes to win.

MCKENZIE: We'll strike tomorrow. *(A beat.)* This makes use sisters.

(McKenzie spits on her hand. Looks over at Samantha, who's grossed out. Samantha shakes her head, then thinks.)

SAMANTHA: The best kind. Sisters of battle.

(They shake hands. Blackout.)

SCENE 7: BATTLEFIELD, VARIOUS

(The dawn before battle. Characters sit on the battlefield, writing home. They're illuminated as they speak.)

RANDY: Dear Mom...

BELLA: Dad, I'm really sorry that—

DREW: It is up with up-most apprehension that I—

HAT-TRICK: Dear Randy's mom,

YVETTE AND ABBY: Tomorrow we like, fight.

BELLA: Despite whatever gruff demeanor we possess, violence eats away at the human soul.

RANDY: I'm scared.

DREW: ...that I admit to apprehension.

HAT-TRICK: No, no. *(Rehearsing it:)* Randy's mom, how's it hangin'?

YVETTE AND ABBY: Chester Drive.

ABBY: That's where it all started.

YVETTE: That's where it's gonna end.

BELLA: McKenzie and Samantha talked battle plans all night.

DREW: The general is in a joyful mood, yet has a maudlin air.

RANDY: I wonder what would happen.

RANDY, DREW, AND BELLA: If I had one in my sights.

BELLA: I'd attack. I'd deaden myself.

DREW: At my heart, I am no soldier.

HAT-TRICK: Missus Randy, I've always found a...a spark. No. Have you seen *The Graduate*?

RANDY: I hate to leave you widowed. Well, except for my brothers. And dad.

BELLA: Don't leave up that photo of me at cheerleading—I hate that picture.

DREW, BELLLA, AND RANDY: In my darkest days,

YVETTE AND ABBY: Hugs and kisses...

HAT-TRICK: Just think about it...

RANDY: Randy.

DREW: Drew.   **BELLA:** Bella.

YVETTE AND ABBY: Yvette and Abby.

(Blackout.)

SCENE 8: OUTSIDE THE HOOPTY BURGER

(The air is overly still. It's a pause, a prelude, or something else, but it isn't fighting. Outside Hoopty Burger, there are a few umbrella tables for outdoor seating, a glass exterior. There are a few specials advertised on it, but they've been covered up with pro-boy propaganda. Samantha, now in a sweeping pink commander jacket with epaulets, steps forward from off right, surveying the site.)

SAMANTHA: No casualties on our side. A rout. As I predicted. Commander?

(McKenzie enters after her.)

MCKENZIE: I've never seen anything like it. Their lines seemed to collapse. A full retreat, sister.

(She looks off the way she came.)

The flag!

(Abby and Yvette emerge, holding the pink flag of girl-kind. They're followed by Bella, who looks weary, traumatized.)

YVETTE: Where do I...

(Samantha removes an umbrella from its stand. Yvette puts the flag in.)

MCKENZIE: All hail Samantha. You should be a four-star general.

SAMANTHA: Not five?

MCKENZIE: I didn't know they went up to five. I meant, like, four out of four.

SAMANTHA: Thank you.

GUILLERMO: *(Off:)* Not so fast.

(The girls turn. Guillermo enters from the left, tossing a

grenade-colored water balloon up and down in his left hand. He's flanked by Randy, Hat-Trick, Drew, and the rest of his army.)

You girls were clever, messing up my supply lines. No ammunition for my sling shots, no rubber bands for my rubber band cannons. You made us retreat. But all isn't lost.

MCKENZIE: *Guillermo.*

GUILLERMO: I still have an equalizer. A single water grenade. Capable of taking you all out at once. Bis peccare in bello non licet. *["It is forbidden to make two errors in war."]*

BELLA: Did you say my name?

(He didn't.)

GUILLERMO: It is forbidden to make two errors in war.

SAMANTHA: You wouldn't throw that.

GUILLERMO: I would, and I will. Samantha, isn't it? The shy guy?

(McKenzie looks suspiciously at Samantha.)

SAMANTHA: Never.

GUILLERMO: The peace treaty...that was you, too?

SAMANTHA: ...Perhaps.

GUILLERMO: When someone is holding a grenade, they deserve better than "perhaps."

SAMANTHA: You used McKenzie up! You got everyone into a war to protect your stupid ego!

MCKENZIE: Guillermo is *not* stupid.

SAMANTHA: She's right, Gui...what? Not?

MCKENZIE: Guillermo is brave and stands up for people.

RANDY: Why is the girl making sense?

SAMANTHA: He's holding a grenade! How is that brave?

GUILLERMO: Silence, all of you. McKenzie?

(McKenzie is about to speak up, when Bella interrupts.)

BELLA: Samantha didn't sabotage any supply lines. She wouldn't have had the chance.

YVETTE: Yeah!

MCKENZIE: Then what was it?

SAMANTHA: Strategy! I was a master strategist.

DREW: I doubt it.

GUILLERMO: *(To his troops:)* I'm the general here. You would all do well to remember that. Nunca talksum.

MCKENZIE: Same goes for me.

SAMANTHA: Well, I think everyone deserves a chance to talk.

MCKENZIE: We could vote on it, then. Who thinks everyone should get to talk?

(Everyone but Guillermo and McKenzie raise their hands.)

I meant all the generals should vote.

BELLA: Why?

GUILLERMO: Because I have a water grenade, and I say so.

BELLA: So you're still in love with McKenzie is what you're saying.

YVETTE, ABBY AND HAT-TRICK: Ooooooh.

GUILLERMO: I am not.

MCKENZIE: Yes you are.

GUILLERMO: Fat chance.

DREW: Did you just call her—

GUILLERMO: No!

(Everyone has moved in closer.)

Give me some space, OK? Space! Alright. Everyone who surrenders, get over to my side, and if you don't surrender, stay over on the girls' side.

(McKenzie makes her way over to Guillermo. No one else moves.)

MCKENZIE: I told you he was fair.

GUILLERMO: Is that it?

SAMANTHA: That's it.

BELLA: You suck, McKenzie.

MCKENZIE: Deal with it.

HAT-TRICK: Wait!

(Everyone looks at him.)

If McKenzie joins our side, then what will they call the other side?

RANDY: The girls?

HAT-TRICK: But we have a girl!

RANDY: He's right, Guillermo.

HAT-TRICK: Thanks Randy!

RANDY: Don't push it.

GUILLERMO: Well, they'd be—

MCKENZIE: The *losers*. The ones who don't know how to get while the getting is good.

GUILLERMO: Oh, Kenzie.

MCKENZIE: The jealous ones who can't appreciate a good boy when they find one.

ALL BUT GUILLERMO AND MCKENZIE: Gross.

(Everyone backs up, away from the fragments of the Girls' Liberation Army, away from the intergender general tryst.)

GUILLERMO: You...?

MCKENZIE: I do, and I will. Ever since the first fire alarm.

(They begin to snog an evil victory snog. As they begin to kiss, Guillermo grips tighter and tighter on the grenade...which explodes, soaking them both. They scream, exiting separately, soaked and defeated. Samantha removes the girl flag and replaces the umbrella. Everyone cheers. Terry and Marie emerge from the restaurant.)

TERRY: You did it, Samantha!

MARIE: I must admit, it was a masterful stratagem.

YVETTE: What was?

ABBY: What's a stratagerm?

(Marie pinches the bridge of her nose, sighs.)

TERRY: You said that people fight because they could. So with Marie's help—

MARIE: I could not resist—

TERRY: I sabotaged all the weapons I could get my hands on.

RANDY: Terry, we trusted you.

SAMANTHA: Why?

RANDY: Because you're a boy. Because of a thing called loyalty. What if Sam had betrayed you?

TERRY: How many people got water ballooned?

(A pause.)

HAT-TRICK: He's a genius!

MARIE: *I* am the — Terry is a very clever individual.

SAMANTHA: And very brave.

(She takes his hand.)

TERRY: And I'd like to declare...peace.

(Cheers!)

RANDY: But girls are still gross.

ABBY: Yeah, whatever. Nice trenchcoat.

HAT-TRICK: They're not as good at kickball, either.

BELLA: You are on, Hat-Trick! See you on the field in ten minutes!

HAT-TRICK: I can get there in five.

BELLA: *(Sprinting off:)* Nuh uh!

(Everyone rushes out, leaving Marie, Terry, and Samantha on stage.)

TERRY: Marie, a moment?

MARIE: Of course. I have to tend to my beep-buzzer anyway...

SAMANTHA: D'Marie, I think you should give kickball a chance. Get some time away from your chemicals.

MARIE: Perhaps. I always had an aptitude for physics.

(She slowly exits, then stops.)

It was a pleasure.

(She gives a brief bow to them, and heads off toward the kickball field. Sam and Terry are alone.)

SAMANTHA: Why?

TERRY: Same question.

SAMANTHA: I asked you first.

TERRY: Fine. Then...how? My "how" was easy.

SAMANTHA: Then start with how.

TERRY: I snuck into a stockpile and took things apart. What I couldn't break, I hid. No weapons, no war.

SAMANTHA: Why the weapons, though?

TERRY: Violence is worse the easier it is. You can fight your fists. But a war needs arms.

SAMANTHA: And a war needs leaders.

TERRY: Which is why you're a general, apparently.

(Samantha begins to take off the jacket. Terry stops her.)

Is it weird to say? It looks good on you.

SAMANTHA: I don't like the person who wears it.

TERRY: I do.

(He moves closer.)

SAMANTHA: Terry, I...

TERRY: What did you say? At Arroyo Hills, at the top of the roller coaster, what did you—

SAMANTHA: That I'd fight for you.

TERRY: And you did —

SAMANTHA: And *you* did —

TERRY: And I will. Whatever it takes —

SAMANTHA: No.   Not whatever it takes.   That's what McKenzie wou —

(And Terry kisses her. And she kisses him. Sam drops her general's jacket. Blackout. End of play.)

APPENDIX 1: Boys & Girls & The Ramifications of Total Warfare

Boys vs. Girls is about a real part of growing up. It's about the difference between being repulsed by the other gender and finding them...oddly interesting. Compelling, even. While that happens at different times for everyone, it's usually in late middle school.

The dialogue is elevated, but that's natural. Part of growing up is about having all the knowledge in the world, but no practical experience. Guillermo has a strong grasp of military Latin, but is upset his girlfriend doesn't like his frog. Samantha and Terry take on issues of global significance. They also have to stop themselves from calling Marie a dweeb.

One thing I cling to in theatre is this; try your best to understand the original writing, because it was almost always slaved over, punchline for punchline, syllable for syllable. But if it sounds overwritten coming out of your mouth, put your own spin on it. Better something that an actor finds meaningful than blind obedience to what's on the page. (Especially if it's an assiduously pronounced typo, which has happened before!)

If you have any script questions, I'd be more than happy to answer them. Please contact me through YouthPLAYS, and I'll get back to you as soon as I can.

-Adam

APPENDIX 2: Cutting for Time

It's entirely possible to perform this show in under 40 minutes. The following cuts will bring you there:

Page 5 can be cut from Hat-Trick's "Didn't hear you..." through his line "next water balloon barrage."

Pages 8-9 can be cut starting at Samantha's "But I have —." Afterwards, Terry would say "You need to dress up as a boy," and throw a pile of clothes at her. Blackout. Her entrance on page 10 would become a sight gag.

Page 11 can be cut from Terry's "Anyway, I thought cooties was just a myth!" to Drew's "What if you want to take your sister, but..." inclusive.

Page 14 can be cut from Yvette's "Not even a little bit in uniform..." to Bella's "You're coming with us" (page 15).

Page 15-16's Retainers can be cut for time or for lack of actors.

Page 21's "pre-scene" can be cut entirely; the scene can start with Terry and Sam entering Marie's lab. If so, excise other references to the lab being under a doghouse (page 21). Also, replace Terry's response to "Because you think I'm a weirdo scientist" (page 23) with "I promise I haven't said that yet."

Page 26 can cut Terry's "Samantha, you're brilliant" and the entire mention of the Beep-Buzzing machine. Instead, end the scene with Marie's line "Scissors. I win."

Page 28-29's "bella/Bella" sequence can be cut. If so, cut it when it when it reappears on page 42.

Page 29 can be cut from Bella's "It's poisoned" to Samantha's "That's good!" inclusive.

The argument that closes Scene 5 cannot be easily truncated, but if you cut the Terry/Sam argument here, make sure to keep both the Samantha/McKenzie argument (which features the Lana Buchanon story) and the final Terry/Sam dialogue.

Page 33-34 can be truncated, with Samantha's line "What happens with no leaders?" leading right to Marie's line "Chaos. Destruction. Cats dressed up as dogs." The scene would then skip to Samantha's "One day, this war's gonna end" and continue to the end.

Page 35: If the retainers were cut on page 15/16, they won't be here as well. Remove their lines.

Page 35: And they won't be on stage to exit here.

Page 37: This scene can end on Samantha's line "And that's really not the point."

Scene 7 can be omitted entirely.

Page 41: The bit after "All Hail Samantha" can be expunged; continue with Guillermo's "Not so fast."

Page 43-44: Bella's reaction ("So you're still in love with McKenzie, is what you're saying") and the following lines until "Give me some space, OK?" can be cut.

Page 44-45: Hat-Trick's question "If McKenzie joins our side, then what will they call the other side?" can be answered with McKenzie's "The *losers*. The ones who don't know how to get while the getting is good."

Page 47: In its simplest form, the scene after everyone leaves to play kickball can be reduced to these lines:

TERRY: You're a general apparently. Is it weird to say, it looks good on you?

SAMANTHA: I don't like the person who wears it.

TERRY: I do.

(*She drops the outfit and they kiss. Blackout. End of Play.*)

The Author Speaks

What inspired you to write this play?
I had just written a bunch of plays myself, and wanted to collaborate with someone. I told my friend Hailey (a girl!) that we'd come up with something, but I came up with an idea before we were able to brainstorm. I never heard back from her, and the story came to me almost instantly. Sometimes the idea just springs on you, which is much easier than when you start at a relationship. A relationship can be anywhere; school kids making war is very specific.

Was the structure of the play influenced by any other work?
Originally, Terry and Sam were more journalistic, riffing on the "Stars and Stripes" section of *Apocalypse Now*. That idea faded almost immediately; it was much more fruitful to have them have personal stakes in the proceedings. That's why it's hard to write journalist characters, frankly: good journalism is objective, dispassionate, and distanced, finding out the truth for someone else's sake. Characters in fiction should have strong—personal—needs.

So either the story isn't important (and it's a tale about the journalist doing an Important Thing), or the journalist isn't important, and you get a kind of *All The President's Men* style procedural.

Have you dealt with the same theme in other works that you have written?
War is new to me. Gender politics are an enmeshed part of writing for and about young audiences. Girls are icky and boys are dumb, there's no getting around it; I could write a hundred years and at the end of it, boys would be dumb and

girls would be icky. It's a building block of the universe, like Avogadro's number.

What writers have had the most profound effect on your style?
I want to shout-out my slam poet friends: Sean Mulroy, Brian S. Ellis, Simone Beaubien, April Ranger, Carlos Williams, Max Kessler, Steve Subrizi, Adam Stone, Harlym 125, Sam Teitel. Prabakar T. Rajan (no one can do what he does), Bobby Crawford, Kevin Spak and Melissa Newman-Evans Spak. Their words have been transformative in how I've turned sentences.

What do you hope to achieve with this work?
This work is a tribute to the dark deities of of Nyl'rateth, who slumber outside of time. Only through children's theatre can they be arisen and swallow our world in their thousand stomachs for all of eternity!

That, and maybe change the way people think about war and social hierarchies in general. Note: the previous sentence's use of "in general" was not meant to be a pun, but it turns out it was.

What were the biggest challenges involved in the writing of this play?
This play wasn't particularly challenging, honestly. Sometimes that's a bad sign; my writing partner and I were coming up with a Lifetime script (called *Neighborhood Cowboy*), and it was really, really easy to write. Then we realized why: the story beats were enmeshed in our culture's thinking. Clichés are easy, archetypes are easy, and if your play is flowing *too* easily, you might be rechanneling what you've already heard.

The ending was originally briefer than the version you see here. Everyone went and played tag or some such; it was too pat.

What are the most common mistakes that occur in productions of your work?
Blind obedience to the page. If a joke doesn't work, jiggle it around. It's like house building; if the ground isn't flat, adapt. If the line doesn't make sense, maybe there's a word missing, or my high-born Massachusetts/Nyl'ratethian accent doesn't translate. I once had a typo in a script that had a phrase as "Did you grow up Calcutta?" instead of "Did you grow up in Calcutta?" That error made it into the final version, because, with 23 other pages to worry about, I simply missed it.

How did you research the subject?
I spent a lot of time around girls, and also boys, then scientists. I watched a bunch of war movies. This play is drawing upon memories and impressions more than specific influences. Perhaps there's a *Naked Gun* bit, or a tad of *Spec Ops: The Line*, *Born on the 4th of July*...I didn't sit down with a history book for this one. I just bunkered down with 200 plus years of American cultural hegemony.

Are any characters modeled after real life or historical figures?
I wrote this play almost immediately after *Sidekickin' It!* was put on, and based the original comedy pair of Randy and Hat-Trick on my friends Griff (who played Von Darkness) and Patrick. Riff died before this or *Sidekickin' It!* got published, but I think he'd be happy with how the part came out. They're naming a scholarship at my alma mater after him, and I can't think of someone more deserving.

Shakespeare gave advice to the players in *Hamlet*; if you could give advice to your cast what would it be?
Have fun with it. Get into the character's head, find out why they do what they do, then do it without an ounce of fear and regret. Fame is admiration for actors who can inhabit someone else so well, we can't tell the difference. Go for it, own it, and make sure you're listening to how your scene partner is playing it. Two great actors will stink on ice if they're playing past each other.

About the Author

Adam J. Goldberg has been creating plays since 2004. He picked up a pen for his school's 24-hour theatre festival, and continued on to Emerson College, where he penned *Sidekickin' It!* (available through YouthPLAYS). He's continued on with a string of hits, including ***The Old New Kid*** (also available through YouthPLAYS), and is currently developing *Very Special Episode: The 80's Sitcom RPG*. He lives in very western Burbank, California.

About YouthPLAYS

YouthPLAYS (www.youthplays.com) is a publisher of award-winning professional dramatists and talented new discoveries, each with an original theatrical voice, and all dedicated to expanding the vocabulary of theatre for young actors and audiences. On our website you'll find one-act and full-length plays and musicals for teen and pre-teen (and even college) actors, as well as duets and monologues for competition. Many of our authors' works have been widely produced at high schools and middle schools, youth theatres and other TYA companies, both amateur and professional, as well as at elementary schools, camps, churches and other institutions serving young audiences and/or actors worldwide. Most are intended for performance by young people, while some are intended for adult actors performing for young audiences.

YouthPLAYS was co-founded by professional playwrights Jonathan Dorf and Ed Shockley. It began merely as an additional outlet to market their own works, which included a substantial body of award-winning published and unpublished plays and musicals. Those interested in their published plays were directed to the respective publishers' websites, and unpublished plays were made available in electronic form. But when they saw the desperate need for material for young actors and audiences—coupled with their experience that numerous quality plays for young people weren't finding a home—they made the decision to represent the work of other playwrights as well. Dozens and dozens of authors are now members of the YouthPLAYS family, with scripts available both electronically and in traditional acting editions. We continue to grow as we look for exciting and challenging plays and musicals for young actors and audiences.

About ProduceaPlay.com

Let's put up a play! Great idea! But producing a play takes time, energy and knowledge. While finding the necessary time and energy is up to you, ProduceaPlay.com is a website designed to assist you with that third element: knowledge.

Created by YouthPLAYS' co-founders, Jonathan Dorf and Ed Shockley, ProduceaPlay.com serves as a resource for producers at all levels as it addresses the many facets of production. As Dorf and Shockley speak from their years of experience (as playwrights, producers, directors and more), they are joined by a group of award-winning theatre professionals and experienced teachers from the world of academic theatre, all making their expertise available for free in the hope of helping this and future generations of producers, whether it's at the school or university level, or in community or professional theatres.

The site is organized into a series of major topics, each of which has its own page that delves into the subject in detail, offering suggestions and links for further information. For example, Publicity covers everything from Publicizing Auditions to How to Use Social Media to Posters to whether it's worth hiring a publicist. Casting details Where to Find the Actors, How to Evaluate a Resume, Callbacks and even Dealing with Problem Actors. You'll find guidance on your Production Timeline, The Theater Space, Picking a Play, Budget, Contracts, Rehearsing the Play, The Program, House Management, Backstage, and many other important subjects.

The site is constantly under construction, so visit often for the latest insights on play producing, and let it help make your play production dreams a reality.

More from YouthPLAYS

The Old New Kid by Adam J. Goldberg
Comedy. 30-40 minutes. 2-9+ males, 3-10+ females (8-30+ performers possible).

It's the half-day of school before Thanksgiving break, and current "new kid" Alan Socrates Bama just wants to get through the day. But when a new-new kid arrives, things change. Alan has three hours to find the meaning of Thanksgiving, survive elementary school politics, battle for his identity, and spell the word "cornucopia" in this *Peanuts*-flavored comedy for kids of all ages.

Herby Alice Counts Down to Yesterday by Nicole B. Adkins
Comedy. 45-50 minutes. 3-7 males, 3-7 females, 4-20+ either (10-50+ performers possible).

Middle school rocket scientist Herby Alice has ambitions as big as the universe, and no time for interviews. Rose Plum, media hopeful, needs a juicy story to get in good with the school broadcast elite. How far is she willing to go to be a star? Or will mad scientists, aliens, befuddled teachers, demanding executives, and the space-time continuum overrun the show?

screens by Jessica McGettrick
Dramedy. 35-45 minutes. 3 males, 7 females, 30 either (10-40 performers possible).

In **screens**, we see the world through the eyes of a gamer, a lonely person looking for love, a music fan, a blogger, a bully's target and many others as they discover the perils and pleasures of creating an online persona that is different from their offline reality. What would you say if no one could see you behind the computer screen? Who would you become?

Miracle in Mudville by D.W. Gregory
Comedy. 60-70 minutes. 5-11+ males, 13-17+ females (21-31+ performers possible).

Casey is the worst ballplayer in the Mudville Little League, the butt of jokes and an embarrassment to his dad, who brags of his glory days in the outfield. But he's not alone in feeling inadequate; his friends suffer by comparison to their parents, too. Then a chance encounter with the ghost of the town's dead librarian throws Casey and his friends into a time warp—where they discover that some of their parents' big adventures didn't quite happen the way they said...

Jennifer the Unspecial: Time Travel, Love Potions & 8th Grade by Matthew Mezzacappa (book and lyrics) & Cynthia Chi-Wing Wong (music).
Musical. 90 minutes. 5-30 males, 3-30 females (8-60 performers possible).

When her science teacher's invention goes horribly wrong, awkward, clumsy eighth grader Jennifer finds herself thrust into a time-traveling adventure with three of her classmates. Through the journey, as they encounter warriors, artists, presidents and love potions, Jennifer discovers she doesn't need anyone's approval to be absolutely amazing and special.

Dear Chuck by Jonathan Dorf
Dramedy. 30-40 minutes. 8-30+ performers (gender flexible).

Teenagers are caught in the middle—they're not quite adults, but they're definitely no longer children. Through scenes and monologues, we meet an eclectic group of teens who are trying to communicate with that wannabe special someone, coping with a classmate's suicide, battling controlling parents, swimming for that island of calm in the stormy sea of technology—and many others. What they all have in common is the search for their "Chuck," that elusive moment of knowing who you are. Also available in a 60-70 minute version.

The Mystic Tale of Aladdin by Randy Wyatt
Fantasy. 50-60 minutes. 9 females.

Seven princesses wait to hear which of them the Sultan has chosen for his bride. To pass the final minutes before he announces his decision, the maidens tell the tale of Aladdin, a tale each claims as her country's own. Filled with magic, adventure, intrigue and romance, this all-female version of the classic story packs a powerful message of empowering young women to fulfill their own wishes.

Long Joan Silver by Arthur M. Jolly
Comedy. 90-100 minutes. 6-15 males, 8-20 females (14-30 performers possible, plus extras).

The classic adventure tale of buried treasure—and the original one-legged pirate with a parrot—gets a timely makeover, combining offbeat farce, sight gags and horrendous puns with a dramatic core that explores discrimination, privilege and greed. Unlike in Robert Louis Stevenson's book, where only one unnamed character is female, women are front and center as ***Long Joan Silver***'s young Jim Hawkins comes of age during the fateful voyage of the Hispaniola and the clash between an all-female pirate crew and Squire Trelawney, Doctor Livesey and the domineering Captain Smollett.

Camp Rolling Hills by Adam Spiegel (music & lyrics), David Spiegel & Stacy Davidowitz (book & lyrics)
Musical. 90-110 minutes. 8+ males, 8+ females (16-50+ performers possible).

When 12-year-old Robert "Smelly" Benjamin is sent away to Camp Rolling Hills, he embarks on the greatest summer adventure of his life—making lifelong friends, breaking the rules, finding first love, and growing up a little along the way.

Made in the USA
Middletown, DE
18 February 2024

49401624R00035